CAT LOVER
Adult Coloring Book

Best Coloring Gifts for Mom, Dad, Friend, Women, Men and Adults Everywhere

GINA TROWLER

Email: gtrowler@colorartwork.com

ISBN-13: 978-1523878000 | ISBN-10: 1523878002

CAT LOVER
Adult Coloring Book

Best Coloring Gifts for Mom, Dad, Friend, Women, Men and Adults Everywhere

GINA TROWLER

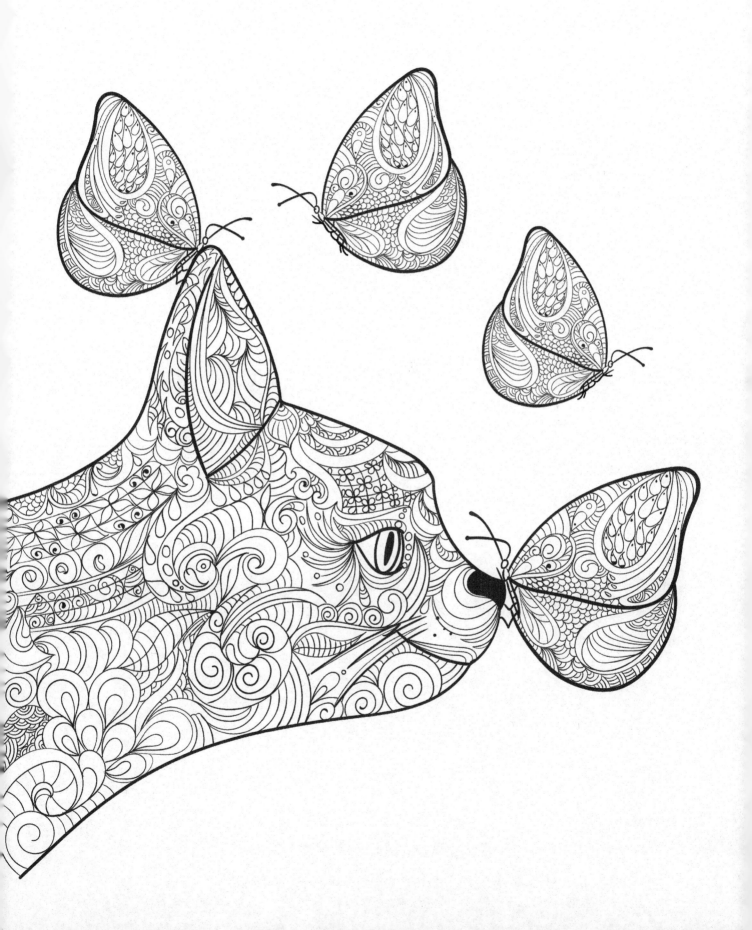

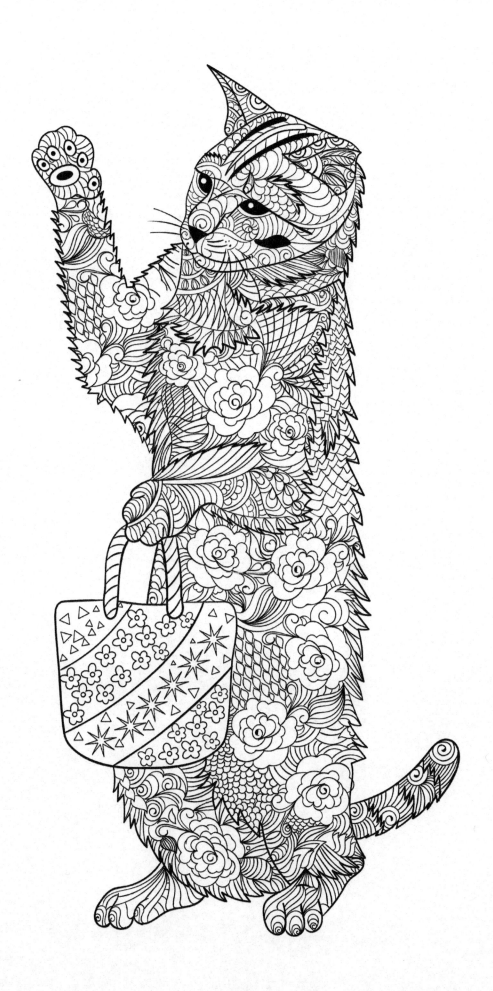

COLORING GUIDE

1. Find a quiet place to do your coloring.

2. Choose your colors according to your liking. Be light and open-minded.

3. Choose to color in bright natural light whenever possible.

4. Make sure you are sitting in a comfortable seat with good back support. Relax.

5. Don't be afraid to express your creativity and imagination in your coloring.

6. Choose your favorite artwork patterns to color.

7. Try to color at a time when you are least likely to be interrupted.

8. If you like music, listen to something soothing while you color.

9. You should consider using coloring pencils over regular crayons.

10. If you prefer art markers, it is best to use a sheet of craft plastic under the coloring page.

11. Take your own time coloring - stop coloring whenever you like.

12. The end result is your own masterpiece.

IMPORTANT:

In order to prevent color-bleeding no images were placed on the opposite side of each artwork printed.

CPSIA information can be obtained
at www.ICGtesting.com
Printed in the USA
LVOW04s0916101117
555775LV00002B/11/P